I0405419

The Proletarianist Manifesto, 3rd Edition

By Karactus Blome

Copyright © 2014 by Karactus Blome

Some Rights Reserved.

The Proletarianist Manifesto may be reproduced and distributed, provided that the following condition is met:

All reproductions of *The Proletarianist Manifesto* must retain the above copyright notice, as well as this condition, and the information below.

Modification of *The Proletarianist Manifesto*, in any form, is strictly forbidden without written consent from the author.
Furthermore, *The Proletarianist Manifesto* may not be sold for profit. Sale of this work at zero profit is acceptable.

PUBLISHER: BLOME, KARACTUS J.
CITY: WHEELING, ILLINOIS, U.S.A.
DATE OF PUBLICATION: DECEMBER 21, 2014

Section I

Has any economic system ever existed that truly favored those who work? I am afraid to say not, for it always seems to pass that the common man and woman are the losers, no matter where you go. Though most economic ideologies aim at creating an ideal society for the commoner, they all fail. To understand why this is, you will need an explanation. I will not disappoint you.

I will begin by examining capitalism. In the ideal capitalist economy, everything (labor, goods, and services) is traded for money, which can in turn be traded for anything else with very little regulation by a governing entity. People who are selling similar goods and services are always in direct competition with one another for customers. The more money you make, the better your quality of life, and the more power you have. Having been raised in a so-called "capitalist" country, I can say that it works to an extent. Everyone works to satisfy their own greed. There in, however, lies the flaw. When people experience the power that comes with having money, they very often abuse it for their benefit, finding ways of

Karactus Blome

manipulating money to make more money. The vast majority of money made in my country (United States) is made from other money, the big central bank where all money comes from is privately owned, and they have the ability to just type trillions of dollars into existence and loan it out. This is a problem, because our currency isn't based on anything valuable, it's based on debt. I can only conclude that someone's greed was responsible for this. To tell you the truth, we are all of us debt slaves. What is even more sad is the fact that most people don't know about this. By the 1930s, capitalism in the United States had decayed into plutocracy, which always favors the elites. There is no way around it. There will always be an elite class and a poor class in capitalism, and as soon as the elite class reaches a certain level of greed (the greedy always get greedier as history has shown), capitalism then decays into a plutocracy. The latter system is what exists in the United States today. Under this rotten system, the government is nothing but a puppet for the elite overlords who are bribing it to pass laws that favor them with no regard to what the people actually want. Many people

The Proletarianist Manifesto, 3rd Edition

begin to be angered by this, so protests will break out when the economy is bad. The elites don't want to lose power, so the government that they already bought and paid for begins militarizing law enforcement and cracks down on the protests. This is the point in which the plutocracy decays into fascism. The protests give the elites an excuse to establish a police state. The people who deny this are part of the problem. I'm watching this happen in my country as I am sitting here writing this! Every time we gather to protest, the police have a new weapon to use against us. Where is the freedom that capitalism promised us now? Long gone. The United States is not the land of the free. In fact, we have the largest prison population in the world. Many prisons are for-profit and privately-owned, and have been lobbying for the politicians to fabricate more laws (reasons to jail people) just to make the prisons more money this whole time. Now, we have a whole bunch of people in jail who don't belong in jail, and the real criminals who should be in jail are the ones running our country.

  I admit that capitalism was fundamentally a good

idea as far as economics is concerned, but look what became of it. Call this a hypothesis of mine if you will; from what I've seen, when you trust the greediest people in your country with the most wealth and power of anyone, it brings out the worst qualities in your leaders. Every man has his price under this system, and even their originally minimalistic government is for sale to the highest bidder, and breeds corruption that leads to the system's decay.

I hate to feel obligated to expose yet another problem with capitalism, but I must do so in order to move forward. What is money? What role does money play in peoples' lives under capitalism, or any of its far more rotten cousins? Originally, money was intended to be nothing more than a means of achieving one's goals. It certainly still serves this function. People work for money, and use the money they earn to achieve their goals and satisfy their wants and needs. The problem arises when we have people hyper-focusing on making money: instead of acknowledging money as a means of achieving a goal, these people actually treat money as the goal, itself. In this way, money is a fetish because it is being made into something it's not. Money is not a thing in and of itself, but a stand-in for another thing. Unfortunately, what happens is that people fall into a trap where they are only looking at the money, and neglecting what actually matters. People are so focused on the dollar amounts, they fail to realize that the resources they need to solve their problems are often right in front of them. They pull out their calculators and try to figure out how profitable each potential solution to their problem is, and then they select the most profitable one, neglecting all other factors but the money involved. This has resulted in many solutions being implemented that are not sustainable or practical. Take the use of fossil fuels for energy as an example. This was chosen as the most profitable solution to our energy problems, but now this has brought a whole slew of new problems for us: fossil fuels are not renewable, and are not a sustainable source of energy. We are eventually going to run out, and when we do, no amount of money will make our gasoline-powered cars run, just because there is no more gasoline. No amount of money is going to light up

Karactus Blome

our power grid then, because there are no more fossil fuels to burn at the plants. To change everything out for renewable energy is going to require energy in the first place; where will this energy come from? Obviously this is a problem, and it happened because people were obsessing over dollar amounts instead of looking at what was staring them right in the face from behind the bank account statements that their eyes were glued to. Many, more sustainable solutions to the problem of meeting energy demands were right in front of those people, but with their eyes glued to the numbers, they failed to see it. They could have used the very same wind that blew around them, or the ambient light from the same sun that illuminated said bank account statements. This is only one example of the problem; since people are always choosing the most profitable ways to solve their problems, it is easy to see how much trouble we could really be getting into down the road. The profitability of a given solution, in no way whatsoever, implies that the solution is a good one, nor does it mean anything in terms of sustainability. To only choose the solutions to our problems that are the most profitable is foolish, incredibly short-sighted, and could potentially doom us in the end when the reality of such an error sets in. Furthermore because capitalists are always doing this to address any problems they face, I suspect that they could make this error numerous times over the course of their nation's lifetime. Needless to say, this is not a good way to decide how to solve problems, and always has the potential to cause more problems later.

My disagreement with capitalists has nothing to do with their ideals, such as freedom and personal responsibility (which are ideas that I support too) but rather with the way that their system is structured to favor a small group of people over the majority, and with the way that their system goes about solving problems, choosing profit over all other factors.

Next, I will discuss socialism. When I speak of socialism, I am referring to a strong, central government featuring high tax rates to pay for the many social programs it runs. This system looks very good on paper, but as history has revealed, it fails in practice. Firstly, if the state taxes the people who work to feed the people who don't, why would you want work in the first place? Secondly, if you have the state requiring every citizen to pay the government part of their income, such an idea implies that the state is enforcing this policy somehow; if the state didn't enforce it, no one would pay. This means that the government is simply taking your hard-earned money by force and using it for their own purposes. In other words, the government functions by robbing citizens while at the same time claiming that it is for "the common good". The citizens cannot truly be assured that the money is even being used for their best interests. Really? If I'm working and you're not working, and the government is robbing me to support you, why is this in my best interests? It isn't. Oh but if I don't pay, they will send their thugs after me with guns to put me in a cage, and if I try to defend myself, they're going to shoot me. That sounds oppressive, doesn't it? That is the problem with a big government. It starts doing the things that it tells us not to do. If you behaved like your government, you'd be arrested.

    This is not to say that I disagree with the ideals of

socialism either; ideals are great, but only if people are motivated to stay true to them. To not work is to not stay true to said ideals. What happened in the more extreme socialist countries (such as the Soviet Union), is that they began employing force to get people to work. People did not want to work on their own initiative, so many of them were sent to forced labor camps. Such situations are not good, either for the people or the government. Nobody ever wants to work if they are being forced, and if they do, they will not likely do a good job, as they don't care about the people they're doing the work for. In the Soviet Union, they soon found this out, and began shooting people who did poor quality work. What does this accomplish? It certainly reduces the number of working age people and therefore damages the workforce that drives one's own economy. Note that the Soviets also did this at the worst possible time, while they were at war with Nazi Germany. Those workers could have been around after the war to help rebuild, but no. They were murdered by their own government during the war because they were not passionate about what they were being forced by their

Karactus Blome

government to do. The Soviets were lucky that their winter saved them when so many of the invading German soldiers froze to death, but diminishing your own workforce by killing them is still no way to win a war.

I have now covered the problems with each extreme in regards to government intervention in the economy. It seems to me that the citizens are not favored in either case. I am at a loss to explain why people think that either of these systems are good for the worker. Neither of them are. I don't care what statistics anyone tries to cite to discredit what I say, because anyone can look at statistics and see what they want to see. Statistics can also be manipulated to show something different than what is actually happening. For example, if I wanted to show that the United States is growing economically, I could look up some U.S. statistics, find a period of time during which it was growing, and cut off all of the other periods of time shown in the study to only show the period during which the United States economy grew. I can then show you only the statistics that I selected and make the claim that the economy got better, when in fact the growth period was nothing but a bubble that then burst immediately after the growth period; I could then say, "The numbers don't lie!", and the vast majority of people wouldn't argue with me. There are all kinds of tricks one can use to manipulate statistics to make people see what you want them to see. This is also why I have not bothered using any statistics to make my arguments. If I showed you any statistics (even if they were not tampered with), you would still have no reason to believe them at all. For that reason, I will not bother with any statistics, nor will I acknowledge any statistics used against me by any opponents; they prove nothing, so I will not waste my time looking at them. If at any time you find yourself in disagreement with me on any topic, your only way to truly show me incorrect is to either make a counterargument or to show that I have misused logic in my argument.

    All of this being said, I will now move forward and actually make my main argument.

Karactus Blome

Section II

If neither capitalism nor socialism are acceptable to me, I suppose you will ask what I propose. In this section, I shall provide you with my answer.

The economic system that I propose shall, as of this moment, be referred to as "proletarianism", and its supporters shall be known as "proletarianists".

A proletarianist country, simply put, is nothing more than a body of workers who all make an agreement with one another that says, "The fruits of my labor will be there for you, if the fruits of your labor will be there for me."

At first, you may wonder what I mean by this. Allow me to explain. The entire workforce in our country shall be composed of workers who volunteer their labor, working on any task of their choice.

Okay, everyone! I hear you! Do I seriously expect everyone to just get up and voluntarily contribute their labor?

Not exactly, because we seek to ensure that one's work is always worth their time. For every hour that a

The Proletarianist Manifesto, 3rd Edition

citizen works, they shall be awarded five hours during which time they will be able to ask whatever they want of other workers, in addition to having the ability to ask for any supplies they need while on the job. For example, if a citizen works for six hours, they will get a total of thirty hours, beginning when they clock themselves out, to have the ability to ask whatever they want from any other workers, and can also ask for any supplies they need to do their job. We will refer to these hours that are awarded as "public trading system hours". Furthermore, any public trading system time not used between work days shall be saved to act as a mechanism of insurance in case anyone needs to take leave from work for any reason.

    Now that I have established the incentive to work in the first place, I am sure there is another question you might ask: what is the worker's incentive to do their job well? This is a question that I am forced to respect. I must, for the answer to this question may immediately decide whether proletarianism will triumph or fail.

    Firstly, every worker must have the right to choose their own profession because in order to do one's job well, one must enjoy the work that they do. Allowing each individual to choose their own profession will accomplish this. Secondly, every worker must be educated so that they will know how to correctly perform the necessary tasks for their chosen profession. For this reason, education in one's chosen profession must be provided (I will discuss the details of education in a bit when it is more convenient). Thirdly, since all labor performed under proletarianism is voluntary, we can assume that workers will be choosing tasks to work on based on their own passions; if you are not motivated to do a good job on any given task, then don't contribute any labor to it in the first place. By providing individuals with the freedom to choose what they want to do, the system ensures that each person is only working for a goal that they are passionate about. Workers will contribute high quality labor because they believe in what they are doing. Otherwise, they would have chosen their career paths differently.

    If you seek evidence for any of the claims I have just made in the last paragraph, look no further than the very fact that this book exists. The copyright on this

The Proletarianist Manifesto, 3rd Edition

document explicitly states that I am not allowed to make any money on it, and I have no plans at all to run for any government office to further the agenda laid down in this book (as I do not believe that proletarianism can be implemented by trying to change any existing system from within), so why would I write it? I voluntarily contributed my labor to put forth this idea, without asking anything in return from anyone, just because I believe in it! That should be all the proof anyone needs to show that proletarianism provides adequate incentive to work, and to do a good job.

    As promised, I shall now explain the functions of the proletarianist education system. I have already established that each individual chooses their profession based on what they enjoy doing. The first function of our education system will be to ensure that the individual is making an educated decision when they choose their line of work. Beginning very early in the education process (as early as elementary education), the students should be introduced to as many different professions as possible. They will learn about what each worker does, why their job is important, and they should be able to list the skills each profession requires. Additionally, students will need an opportunity to discover what their own talents are in order to make an educated decision about their professions. This can be done by providing the students with a general sampling of the skills that are commonly used in the various professions. This includes basic mathematics, language, science, and many others. The science that is learned in elementary school will mostly apply to agriculture and geography (Earth science). The students should also be able to practice their skills (and determine if they possess the gifts needed for the very labor-heavy jobs) if the teachers assign them certain tasks on a nearby farm or mine. The purpose of our elementary school system is to allow each student to determine for themselves if the path of the farmer, miner, or logger is right for them. If not, the student might not do very well in elementary school. This is okay. We do not interpret grades the same way that they traditionally have been interpreted. To us, a low grade means nothing in terms of being a good student or a bad one. Instead, earning a low grade in one subject or another only serves as an indicator that the subject is not one's strong point.

Each person has different gifts and talents. Some people are motivated to be physically engaged, while others are of a more intellectual nature. The jobs that require more muscle and less intellect will be immediately available to students following their completion of elementary school, in the form of an apprenticeship. All students will have a choice to either accept an apprenticeship or to continue school. This means that the least intellectually-driven people will be immediately siphoned off into the workforce after elementary school because they are not intellectually-motivated enough to continue school, so there is no point in forcing anyone to do so. This is convenient because the professions that require less intellect and more muscle, such as farming, mining, and logging (to name a few), happen to be very critical in any economy. We must be sure that there are always workers in those professions, and that said workers are happy so as not to encourage any labor strikes. If these workers go on strike or if there are not enough of them, there will be huge problems, so we had better keep them happy so that they will always be willing to supply us. Remember that these workers are volunteers like everyone else, and they are under no obligation to help us if we mistreat them.

Before I carry on, there is a point that I feel needs to be made to prevent you from getting the wrong idea: the job that one holds, by no means at all, says anything about their social status. A true proletarianist is mature enough to acknowledge that all people are gifted in at least one way, and that everyone's talents are useful in our economy. We will not look down on those who do not continue education past elementary school, because those are the people who are going to be providing the most critical resources in the economy. Remember that if it wasn't for the farmer's decision to abandon school for an apprenticeship, you would inherently have less food on your table when you entered the workforce later. The point that I am attempting to make here is that not a single person should ever be considered expendable. Things are expendable, people are not. Keeping that in mind, realize

The Proletarianist Manifesto, 3rd Edition

that safety needs to be one of the highest priorities for masters to teach and practice with their apprentices, as they are the new generation of workers and cannot be replaced if anything happens to them.

    Once elementary school is completed, the student should have an idea of whether or not a low-intellect profession suits them. The middle stage of childhood education shall focus on developing each student's gifts. For the least intellectually-driven people, this middle stage of education is an apprenticeship; everyone else continues school to develop their mental skills for higher-skilled professions. All of the basic subjects, such as mathematics, language, and science, that the students learned in elementary school are expanded on. Students will also be able to choose electives to investigate different lines of work. After completing the middle stage of their education, a new tier of apprenticeships becomes available, which are more intermediate professions. The difference between this tier of professions available to graduating middle school students and the professions available to graduating elementary students is that these careers require more intellectual skills. Some of the professions on this tier may include carpentry, construction, plumbing, and others. These careers require skills such as geometry, basic algebra, and some very basic chemistry and physics that one learns in middle education, but not in elementary school. Just as with elementary school, the middle school graduates have a choice between accepting an apprenticeship and continuing school, so some of the students who graduate middle school will again be siphoned into the workforce as apprentices in the lines of work that I mentioned above, depending on what they choose to do.

    The next level of education after middle school, also known as high school, introduces higher levels of mathematics and science. High school students are again able to choose between many electives to explore the careers that will be available to them immediately after graduation. These should include (but not be limited to) engineering science (the people who enjoy these classes will likely be our inventors who design everything in our country and create new technology), metallurgy science

The Proletarianist Manifesto, 3rd Edition

(the people who enjoy these classes will be our metallurgists and our smiths who forge all of the larger metal products that we will use), education (obviously, these people are going to be our teachers, but they will need to specialize in one of the stages of education), computer science (these people will be our programmers, computer technicians, and computer manufacturing workers), high tech manufacturing and robotics (these people will be our high-tech factory machinists), military (the people who enjoy military-oriented classes will likely be our soldiers), and theoretical science (for all of our young Einsteins, who will be exploring all the depths of science for knowledge to pass onto our inventors and engineers to create new technology from; they will however, need to continue their education even further after high school). As you can see, high school is when students begin to specialize themselves by choice of electives once they find a career path they enjoy in the tier of professions after high school. There should also be proletarianist economics and history electives. People who enjoy these classes will be the ones who do all of the work

Karactus Blome

behind the scenes to make sure that the economic system itself is functioning at all times. Whenever anyone begins working in the profession they choose, they will need to visit the economic administrators who register everyone. Once registered new workers are then free to volunteer their labor for any task or project that involves their profession that they believe in, and be rewarded for it.

If a student goes through high school, and still doesn't seem to enjoy any of the subjects taught in high school, then there are a few lines of work left over that they are able to try, which include the arts, medicine, and philosophy. These are the fields taught in higher education along with advanced theoretical science. Our scientists and artists will very likely be career students in addition to their jobs, studying whatever interests them while the doctors graduate in a few years to intern at hospitals and the like, and eventually practice medicine.

By explaining how our entire education system would work, I have now also given you a glimpse of what our economy would actually look like: every person is volunteering their labor for things they believe in, and the

The Proletarianist Manifesto, 3rd Edition

whole end goal of the proletarianist economic system is its own advancement and improvement.

Now, to answer the question of how we should structure all of our living communities. Let us consider what our goal is: our own economic growth as a nation. We can make it easier to accomplish this by building our communities in strategic places for certain natural resources in the country. Each community should have, at the very least, a farm with enough land to feed everyone with a surplus, a school for each stage of education, a local economic administration office to register new workers, a power plant, a medical center, and a nearby army base for protection. In addition, the communities are going to specialize their production based on the natural resources immediately available to them. These communities will need a lot of room to grow, due to population increases, so they will need to be spaced accordingly. Road systems will be needed to connect all of the communities. Because our society will be aimed at creating a high work incentive, many of the workers might have their work facilities built into their houses just to

Karactus Blome

make it more convenient for them to work. A carpenter might have a room dedicated for woodworking, and a smith might have a room that is dedicated as a forge. Many people might be working from home if they have children to worry about, but still want to be able to participate. The living communities must accommodate the volunteers comfortably, and will be built specifically to do so. Once the economic administrators get down the science of planning the communities correctly, communities might just be mass-constructed in clusters near each other, making the most economically efficient use of all of the nation's land as possible with each community specializing in making products from specific resources based on which natural resources are available nearby. Due to the need for overproduction, our entire nation will likely be designed and zoned in this manner, with huge swaths of land allocated for the production of any sustainable natural resources of utility on it. The natural resources are obtained by the workers who have been trained to do so. They are working for the time to ask whatever they want of anyone else. The economic administrators are responsible for maintaining the system that keeps track of everything in the economy, and for providing the medium both for the trade of labor for time, as well as requests by individuals with time for help or supplies from others. Every single volunteer who contributes their labor shall be registered in a database that lists everyone under their profession (determined by the job they chose to train for), and whenever someone asks for a task or a project to be done, everyone who is listed under the professions the request concerns will see the task or project as an option on their computers. They can choose to accept the task, but they don't have to if the project does not interest them or if they don't agree that it is a good use of resources. This means that things will only happen if enough people think that it is a good idea. The inventors design new things, and then they have to pitch their ideas by asking other people if they would be willing to get the resources they need to put their designs into production. If those other people think the inventors have good ideas, they will certainly get a lot of help. However, if what someone proposes is a horrible idea that no one else likes, then chances are it just won't happen due to a lack of manpower or supplies. Construction workers need to be recruited to build whatever facilities are needed for the inventors' ideas, all the workers who produce what the facilities need will also need to be recruited to supply it, and finally we will need workers who are willing to staff these facilities. Everyone is simply encouraged to follow their passions and work for whatever change they want to see. They will also be given everything they need in order to do so, assuming enough of the other workers are in agreement that the effort is for a just cause. The medium on which all of this happens shall be known as the Public Trading System, provided by our economic administrators who volunteer their time and effort to maintain it, and with help from our computer scientists who volunteered their time to write the software we need for this system and to build the necessary computer systems. After all of this is set up, there should be very little need to change it. To protect our system from being hacked from the outside, our country must have its own internet, isolated from the rest of the world. There shall be

The Proletarianist Manifesto, 3rd Edition

no network connections running between our public trading system and the capitalist world, for the sake of our own economic integrity. This also makes it more difficult for our enemies to determine what our military would be armed with because no statistics about our economy will be available to them.

What do the economic administrators do, exactly? They are responsible for deciding how land will be allocated in each community, as well as performing the record-keeping involved in the public trading system. This is because we trained them to know how to do this. We are simply putting the economists where they belong, and making their opinions matter.

I have often been asked by my opponents who pays for the public trading system. In the context of proletarianism, such a question makes no grammatical sense at all. We don't bother measuring anything in terms of monetary value, so to ask "who pays for..." is completely nonsensical. This is not to say that we have no concept of value, but we do not use money to measure it. We leave the task of measuring value to each individual, because the individual is responsible for prioritizing their own labor contributions. Each person will give higher priority to whatever is valuable to them, and everyone will work according to their own priorities. If enough people consider the achievement of any one goal to be valuable, it will be achieved (or at least attempted), end of story.

How do we decide who owns what and how to divide our resources? Ownership is extremely simple under proletarianism: you own yourself, your house, everything in it, and any product you ask for on the public trading system; nobody owns anything else. We will not acknowledge any claims of ownership in regards to land or the natural resources on it. The Earth, the land, and the resources have existed for far longer than humans have, and it is not a human right to carve up the land or to divide up the resources on said land. Anyone who tries to make such an arrogant claim as one of ownership better be ready to defend it. First of all, no one else is going to acknowledge their claim. Second of all, our army will see any claim of land ownership as a foreign invasion, and they will see any claim of natural resource ownership as theft. The army will respond accordingly in either case.

I hear you, objector. Doesn't that take away our freedom?

Not at all. From the eyes of one of our people, the land that makes up our country isn't owned, it simply exists. The natural resources on the land are not owned, they simply exist. The use of land and natural resources is determined directly by the public trading system in accordance with the priorities of each individual who voluntarily participates in it. In other words, the more people involved who assign a given project a high priority, the more resources we will spend on said project as a natural consequence of more people being willing to go out and obtain the resources needed to work on it.

Again, I hear another objection. "I want a big mansion with a thousand rooms and a fleet of two-hundred luxury cars just because I want it!!!"

Wow! Getting greedy, are we? Well technically, no one is stopping you from having all of those things, but good luck getting people to volunteer for such a project. I doubt anyone else will be passionate about wasting so

Karactus Blome

many resources on one person, especially all at once. If people are so inclined to want big houses, then I suggest we specifically design our homes to be vertically modular, by which I mean having each floor of every house be one standard module that attaches to the floors above it and below it. This means that any house can be made into a bigger house by detaching the roof module, attaching another floor module on top, and then reattaching the roof above the new floor module. Then the owner of the house can do whatever they want with the new floor. Naturally, we can make this even easier by standardizing the size of all of the houses we build to match the size of our modules so that any module can go on any house or foundation. This will also allow us to predict exactly how much land we will need to house everyone in a given community if all houses have the same size foundation. If you want a bigger house, no problem! You don't even need to move; we'll just add another floor to your existing house so you'll have a bigger house, and we don't even have to worry about using more land. Everyone wins that way. Problem solved. As for the fleet of two-hundred luxury cars, well

The Proletarianist Manifesto, 3rd Edition

sorry but no one is going to want to just volunteer to make you two-hundred luxury cars. We have far better things to do with our resources. Try asking for one at a time every few months, and people will probably be a lot more interested in helping you. After a few years, your collection might start to look impressive, but no one will ever have everything they want all at once. Remember that although every worker certainly has the incentive (public trading system hours) to work on any project, each one will be prioritizing their own tasks based on what is important to them. This means that while they'll be happy to help make sure that everyone has a car in their driveway, the workers understand that someone who asks for two-hundred of the best cars in the nation and wants them all at once clearly doesn't understand the scarcity problem (either resource scarcity or labor time scarcity). The workers will be weighing how long each of their potential tasks will take; the workers at the car factory could either expend all of the resources and time needed to make two-hundred cars for one person (which we all know is a ridiculous waste), or they could expend the

Karactus Blome

same amount of time and resources to make two-hundred cars for two-hundred different workers who have each only asked for one, but who have all earned the time to ask for a car. If that were you in the factory, which would you choose? To make such a ridiculous request as the former would not be illegal, but it would be extremely inappropriate to be certain.

Moving on, I am now going to discuss defense. The army has been mentioned a few times already, I believe. We have yet to discern how the army will be organized, who will lead it, and how it will be supplied. I intend to answer these questions now. To have an army, even if it is only a defensive force, is essential. Others in the international community might be jealous of what we have, which obligates us to defend ourselves.

The army will function differently than any other. All of our soldiers will have joined the army voluntarily, and the profession of "soldier" shall be treated in a similar fashion to any other job, with a difference: soldiers are always able to request things on the public trading system as long as they are in service due to the fact that the soldier is considered to always be "on the job" while they are in the military. Our equivalent of veteran benefits shall be the awarding of five public trading system hours for every hour that soldiers spend serving the country, beginning as soon as they retire from the military. So for every day that a soldier serves, he/she gets the credit for working twenty-four hours, and when multiplied by five, this comes out to five public trading system days awarded for every single day that the soldier spends in the service, and the soldiers do not even begin using this public trading system time until they leave the military. Now if you reckon up the sheer number of public trading system hours a soldier will accumulate over the course of their entire military career, you will immediately know that this will ensure that anyone who risks their life for the safety of our people shall be properly compensated for it. Many veterans will likely need not ever work again. This is intentional. We believe that it would not be right to ask anything more of our veterans after their time in the service. Veterans will still be free to volunteer more of their labor if they choose to, but they have so many public

Karactus Blome

trading system hours already that they likely won't have to. The reason we create such a high incentive to serve in the military is because we need to take our defense very seriously. Any foreign invaders would find themselves facing a very large, and professional military force whose only purpose is to defend our people with the most advanced weapons our inventors can come up with.

Most soldiers in our country shall be career soldiers. During peacetime, the only thing the soldiers will ever be doing is training, practicing, and enhancing their fighting skills. Each individual soldier gets their weapons by asking for whatever weapons they want that are available on the public trading system. If the weapon they want is not currently available, they can put forward a request to the inventors to come up with something new that suits their needs. No one is in charge of the army. It is up to the soldiers with more seniority to train newcomers. During peacetime the army trains and fortifies, just waiting for a foreign country to be stupid enough to attack us. As soon as we are attacked, the soldiers get a free run of the country to kill as many enemies as they can. The

The Proletarianist Manifesto, 3rd Edition

soldiers will use whatever technology the public trading system has to offer to smash our enemies into dust. There is no real organization to the army, other than seniority generally leads due to experience. Newcomers certainly ought to listen to the more experienced veterans who have already been in the field. They don't have to, but a natural consequence of not doing so will be death if they don't listen and end up getting themselves killed somehow.

In layman's terms, all the army does is train and train and train, and wait for someone to attack. When the country is attacked, all of the soldiers just grab their favorite guns (or perhaps whichever guns they think will be most useful to them) and go shoot up the invaders. Crude, but effective. The reason this is effective is because of the extremely high incentive to join the military. Our army is likely to be many millions of people strong (depending on how big the country is), just because of the high incentive to serve. All of those soldiers are going to hand-pick their own weapons based on what they think is useful to them. If you invade our country, we will not be sorry for the fact that millions upon millions of

Karactus Blome

professional soldiers will be trying to kill you, and they will be using the best weapons we can arm them with. You will find those soldiers within and behind the best fortifications we are able to build (if you even make it that far), and if you do, they will kill you. You're going to die either way if you attack us, so just don't. It's a bad idea. As far as the international community is concerned, we will always be as quiet as a mouse. You will not hear anything from us as long as you stay out of our country. We don't care about anything that happens outside of our borders unless it directly affects us in some way. If you don't bother us, we won't bother you.

Additionally, civilians should also be allowed to bear whatever weapons are available on the public trading system that suppliers are willing to give them.

War will not be the only aspect of our foreign affairs. Capitalists shall be welcome to enter our country with intentions to trade and sell us their goods, but we will pay for everything in public trading system hours, and we will only trade for something if we will find it useful. Prices can be negotiated to everyone's satisfaction.

The Proletarianist Manifesto, 3rd Edition

However, the establishment of any private companies within our borders will offend us. Outsiders shall not be permitted to use any natural resources in our country, unless they do it through the public trading system by trading for time to access the resources they want. Those who violate this principle will expect the army to use the company's facilities as target practice, as we will assume you are up to no good; not only are you claiming ownership of our land, which we explicitly stated that nobody can own, you are also stealing and using our resources, which we said could only be used through our economic system. The army defends the principles of the system. Now, the army isn't actually going to attack these companies in an organized manner like they would a foreign army. Instead, some soldiers might be out exploring and might happen on a private company while they are out. They will not recognize it as one of ours, because our buildings will all be built together in communities. The soldiers will immediately know it isn't supposed to be there, and if they're bored and want something to shoot at, they will be happy to know that

Karactus Blome

firing on the company isn't illegal. They might use it as target practice. Those won't be our citizens in that company they're shooting at, because our citizens will never need to seek employment through capitalism, ever in their lives. No. Those are foreign companies, and they must have brought their own employees to our country to work. That means they are fair game; they went well out of their way to knowingly violate the principles of our economy, and they will suffer the consequences of doing so. Regardless, I highly doubt any capitalist private companies will ever want to set up shop in our country to begin with, mainly because we don't use the same kind of currency, and nobody will acknowledge any claim they make to own anything in our country. It won't be profitable, so they probably won't anyway. I wouldn't worry about it.

    Our border will consist completely of anti-vehicle obstacles. This means that pedestrians are free to cross into our country at will, but their vehicles must stay behind. These vehicles could be cars or they could be tanks for all we care, but they're not getting in here either

The Proletarianist Manifesto, 3rd Edition

way. When I say "anti-vehicle obstacles", I am referring to huge anti-tank obstacles like Czech hedgehogs, and they will be set up along all of our borders by the army to keep enemy vehicles out. This is a very defensive strategy. If we are attacked, enemy infantry can march right past the border, but the tanks will be stopped dead in their tracks. That is the reason for this. The army will probably also have unarmed scouts in disguise patrolling the borders, so that they can tell us if a foreign army is gathering at the border. If there is, the scouts run back and report it at the nearest base, and then the soldiers will go and do their jobs. The army will likely have all kinds of technology at its disposal to detect an attack. Our strategy will involve trying to negate as many of our enemy's technological advantages as possible. If we can restrict the enemy's avenues of attack (land, air, sea, etc) and force them to fight a conventional land war with infantry only, we will have an advantage. This is how we will fight wars: we will put many of our inventors to work on building systems that will negate enemy air power (I believe Nikola Tesla came up with one such system that would allow us to

Karactus Blome

simply throw a lightning bolt at anything in the sky we don't like, so there's one idea), and we will also work on weapon systems that will just make our enemies think twice about invading us in general. Also, just because we will be quiet on the world stage doesn't mean we will not be listening. We will pay attention to world current events, so I'm sure we will know if someone has a reason not to like us.

Now that defense is over with, we can see everything coming together. There is one more question to address: who makes laws? The answer is no one. Proletarianism does not require any regulation. Our system has principles, not laws. These principles do not change. There is no mechanism to change them. They will never require revision.

Yes, I know that many people might object to what I just expressed in the last paragraph. I will respond to the objections at a later time when it is more convenient. Let's carry on for now.

Section III

Now that I have provided an overview of this new ideology, there are some specifics I need to talk about.

I have mentioned some principles in the last section, and I realize that I have neglected to explicitly say what these principles are. I will do so.

The first principle of our economy shall be sustainability. If we are going to build a nation for ourselves that serves us, we want it to be able to serve us for thousands of years to come. We will not waste our time with resources that are not renewable, because it is never a worthwhile investment of labor. In the long run, a sustainable system will serve us far better than profit ever will. Do not violate this principle, as capitalism has done. The consequences of doing so will be dire for everyone concerned. This principle isn't enforced by humans, but by nature herself. Violators will suffer the natural consequences if they make this fatal mistake, for it will spell doom for everyone in their country. There is nothing more that needs saying. Anyone who takes an economics class will immediately know that the problem with unsustainable practices goes without saying.

I suppose you might ask what alternatives I suggest to fossil fuels, while we're on the topic. If it were up to me, I would choose hemp as our main energy resource; hemp is sustainable. Firstly, we can grow as much hemp as we want. Secondly, we can grow hemp virtually anywhere. Thirdly, we can make bio-fuel from hemp. Hemp grows quickly. Producing bio-fuels from hemp could completely break any country's dependence on fossil fuels.

Yes capitalist objectors, I hear you. Hemp will put a lot of other industries out of business.

We're sorry to hear that, but it isn't our problem. We chose not to pursue development of said other industries in the first place. Fortunately for you, we can make tissues out of hemp; take some tissues and go cry about it.

Do you remember my criticism of capitalism that it never seems to think much of sustainability? It is one of our primary principles. We must strive to make the most use as possible out of the resources we will always have.

The Proletarianist Manifesto, 3rd Edition

Thus we shall recycle all of our metal objects that are used for work when they break, and they should all be given back over to metallurgists to be melted down. We will do everything in our power to keep our economy as sustainable as possible.

The second principle of our economy shall be mutual friendship and the collaboration of all workers. We must strive to cultivate friendship among all of our people. Make no exceptions to this principle. We all want an economy that serves us, and to accomplish such a feat requires that we all stand together. Though each worker may have different goals, and may contribute their labor to different causes, the proletarianist world shall stand together in solidarity for the cause of the freedom and the power that we have worked so hard to earn for ourselves. We will raise our fists high in the air at anyone who tries to take what we have built away from us!

Yes objector, once again I hear you. Where is the competition? We need competition for a healthy economy.

We agree! Allow me to set up a scenario that will illustrate how competition works under proletarianism.

Karactus Blome

Suppose we have two inventors who each come up with a different idea regarding how to solve the same problem, and both ideas have some level of support from the professions involved. This will not result in any real economic consequences for either side if one idea wins over another; it is more or less a friendly competition for bragging rights. Each faction in this competition will of course be free to work on their ideas. Each solution to the problem will be observed to see how well it works. If one solution works better than another, then certainly we should expect this to become apparent in some way. When it does, whichever solution works better to solve our problem will become more widespread as it will seem to be a better idea, and the other idea less so; let the best solution win in any case.

Our third principle is voluntarism and mutual nonaggression. We do not believe in the use of force against one another. Such practices are moronic and damaging to our own economy. Anyone who violates this principle shall find many other workers refusing to accept tasks from them. We do not need to create a system of

The Proletarianist Manifesto, 3rd Edition

checks and balances, because our economic system already comes with them built in. Those who use force will likely be boycotted. Our boycott is of a different form than its capitalist equivalent. Rather than refusing to ask for products or services from the target of our boycott, we will instead refuse to serve the target of our boycott. In other words if you threaten or mistreat the farmer, the farmer can refuse to feed you. Pulling a gun and ordering the farmer to give you food will not work. It only takes one person to make a trip to the nearest army base and report it, and the robbers will soon find soldiers chasing them out of our country, if they don't just shoot the robbers outright. Not to mention that since we support the idea of an armed populace and the right to bear arms, even an armed civilian might just shoot the robbers and save soldiers the trouble.

    I hear an objection from the left-wing this time: all this talk of guns is making proletarianism seem barbaric and uncivilized.

    It really isn't. Threatening your fellow citizens with a gun in the first place is barbaric. Violating the principle

Karactus Blome

of nonaggression is barbaric. Stealing is barbaric. Thinking that you can make your way in our society (or any other for that matter) by threatening others and stealing from them is barbaric. Thus logically, for a government to ban or try to regulate guns and enforce it with a threat is also barbaric, and we will not tolerate that either. If you want to live in our society, you will behave in a civilized manner according to our principles. If you don't, and end up being shot because you decided to engage in the aforementioned barbaric practices, we will not feel sorry for you. In this regard, we would seem to have some common ground with anarchists. Indeed, we also resent statism for its use of force against the populace. We don't care who you are or what you want, but if you use force to try to impose your will on us, you will find even more force being used to drive you out of our country.

    We are not worried so much about our citizens using guns on each other, as we try our very best to cultivate friendship among our people. I know some people might not like one another, but if you're going to

The Proletarianist Manifesto, 3rd Edition

pull a gun on any of your fellow workers just because you don't like them, then you're not one of us. If you don't think you are personally mature enough to handle living with us, then please just don't. It's really that simple.

Now, recall that at the end of the last section, I made statements expressing that proletarianism does not require regulation. Now I will explain exactly why, since we are on the topic.

In any country with a government that claims to have freedom of expression, people who are opposed to a given idea petition their government to pass a law against it. The government's legislative branch then votes on the proposal and supposedly the majority rules. If the law passes, the government then pays thugs with guns to force its decision on everyone else in the name of "the common good" or "morality".

Proletarianism also has a mechanism for dealing with issues like unpopular or unethical ideas, but it is of a different nature. Instead of having a government just make a decision and then force everyone else to go along with it, proletarianism addresses this problem by empowering every single individual to boycott (by which I mean our form of boycott) anything they believe to be unethical. If you don't like people doing something, then you don't have to work for it, nor do you have to supply them with the materials they need to continue their unethical practices. Just work on some other tasks instead to get your hours. If enough of your fellow workers agree with you, then the practitioner(s) of the unethical actions will likely be forced to stop their practices due to either a lack of supplies, manpower, or both.

The reason why proletarianism deals with these issues far more effectively than a state becomes apparent when you consider each system's method.

Laws are only effective on people who follow them. Those who don't will still engage in said unethical practices. A law doesn't stop a criminal from committing murder, robbery, drug or human trafficking, or anything else that is generally considered to be unethical. There is nothing physically stopping criminals from doing what they want; the only thing a law really does is label them as criminals in the first place so that the government's hired

The Proletarianist Manifesto, 3rd Edition

guns know who to go after.

However, suppose you were to try to engage in such activities under proletarianism. Workers who disagree with your practices will immediately initiate their boycotts and refuse to serve you. If enough of them are in agreement that your actions are unethical, then you will be rendered physically incapable of carrying on your unethical activities due to a lack of supplies or manpower. Since I have already stated that any attempt to rob our workers will be met with deadly force (if necessary) from either armed civilians or the military, this should be more than enough to ensure that unethical activities are discontinued if enough people are in agreement that the activities are indeed unethical.

After realizing this, you will now know and recognize that proletarianism deals with ethical problems far more effectively than other systems ever will. You cannot carry out any actions without the supplies you need, nor can you do so without workers.

I can think of one last objection that might be stated on this matter: instead of using force to steal

Karactus Blome

supplies for unethical practices, they can use stealth. This is easily negated. As you might expect, everything that happens on the public trading system can be logged, and should be. If a practitioner of unethical practices seems to be unaffected by a boycott, this can be challenged because an economic administrator can be asked to pull logs from the public trading system to see if they contain any record of the practitioner obtaining the supplies legitimately; even if capitalists came into the country and sold the practitioner supplies in exchange for public trading system hours (this is also considered legitimate), there would be record of the transaction because public trading system hours would have been transferred from the practitioner to said capitalists, who would have a new guest entry created for them in the database for their time. If not, it can be assumed that the supplies were stolen. If this is the case, the practitioner's citizenship will be revoked on the grounds of principle violation, and they will no longer be subject to our principle of nonaggression, or any other principle for that matter. Activists will then be able to take any action they

The Proletarianist Manifesto, 3rd Edition

wish against the practitioner, as no citizenship means no protection from the army. If the logs indicate that the practitioner legitimately obtained what they needed through the public trading system, then we can assume that there were not enough people boycotting the practitioner, and thus the issue should be dropped because the consensus seems to be in favor of the practice. If opposition to the practice later gains more support, then the practitioner can be challenged again at a later time if their practice continues despite boycotts.

    The next principle is overproduction of all essential goods. This principle requires no further support. Everything about this system encourages overproduction to begin with by allocating land strategically for the resources on it, teaching the most vital professions in school before anything else to ensure that there are always a sufficient number of laborers to overproduce essential goods, and implementing the most sustainable and efficient methods of production to ensure we can always have a standing supply on-hand to work with. There is also a great bounty of incentive to work, and to do one's job well. Thus, I think it is safe to say that overproduction goes without any further support.

With these principles, I have constructed an entirely new economic system that has never existed before. Its goal is to serve the proletarian without the use of force or the presence of oppression, hence I have named it Proletarianism.

Section IV

We must now discuss how to put this system into practice. Recall from Section II, when I expressed my disbelief in the idea that proletarianism could be achieved by changing any other system from within. This is because we cannot elect any officials we can trust with the power to tell us what to do.

You need to ask yourself what you want to do. You could sit here your whole life trying to vote people in and hope they don't go corrupt and screw you over. All the while, this government is robbing you of your hard-earned money and threatening to throw you in a cage if you don't give them said money (if you try to defend yourself when they come to throw you in a cage, they will shoot you). We can't do this from the inside.

Instead, we must break off from this society to form our own together. We will be a stateless nation. There shall not be a true political party in our name. We will act as a leaderless movement. Everyone should know the principles to follow. We need to get together, all of us, and build our own communities. We will refuse to work for the old system, and begin working for our own. The more support we get from the populace, the more difficult it will be to uproot the movement. We will abandon the old system entirely. When we have all united together, we shall abandon money, and the capitalist economy that existed in our country will diminish with every person who joins our movement.

Soldiers, I am sure that you deserve far more than what the capitalists pay you, even in benefits after you leave the service. No, you have risked making the ultimate sacrifice for our freedom. I know that freedom is something that most human beings hold dear. What would you say if I told you that we hold freedom in even higher regard than the capitalists do? We are speaking of breaking free of all our limitations, either monetary or otherwise. Soldiers, if you worked for us you would be able to have any guns you want. Your benefits would consist of being able to ask for anything whenever you want during your time in the service and for several decades after. If you think you need a tank to beat the invaders, I'm sure we will have inventors and engineers

The Proletarianist Manifesto, 3rd Edition

who are willing to just design you a tank that suits your needs, just because there are people who are passionate about inventing war machines and hold their freedom in high regard. You will even own that tank yourself, because your labor kept us free to design it and make it in the first place! We will always give you the best weapons we can come up with, and you wouldn't be limited by a budget. If you want a 0.50 caliber machine gun that shoots 1200 rounds per minute that can fire all day, I'm sure our volunteers can help you get a monster machine gun because that is what some inventors like to do, and they value their freedom and will work to keep it at all necessary costs. You would also own that machine gun once we begin mass production after initial tests. Staffing the production facilities and supplying them should not be a problem. We will then be able to put it into production, because we have a lot of people who are interested in keeping their freedom who would likely be willing to staff the facility and supply the factory in exchange for the time to ask whatever they want of other workers. Simply sign onto the system we create, and enter yourself as a soldier.

Karactus Blome

Those who do not wish to be warriors shall of course be our workers. They are also able to become soldiers at any time after high school if they wish to serve our country at any later point in time, but no one is ever obligated.

Fellow volunteers who wish to join our movement, this is it. I am sending out the first request to anyone who acknowledges the public trading system time that I should have acquired by writing this book and putting forth the idea: build the public trading system. This request involves our supporters who know computer science. Build us the computers and/or write us the software we need to initiate the public trading system, and when all of the other volunteers sign onto it and the system goes into action, we will make sure that you are more than compensated for your time and effort. It is okay if you work for capitalists to get money and buy this computer system from them at this beginning phase, as we have not diminished capitalism yet. Either way, we are awaiting the completion of this vital task for the establishment of proletarianism in our country.

The Proletarianist Manifesto, 3rd Edition

By signing on, all you are doing is saying that you would be willing to volunteer to make this system happen. We can break off from the old society as soon as we have enough people. We don't need everyone to go along with it, only enough of you. We will build this new society together, and we will teach the capitalists a thing or two about how simple economics can be if we eliminate all of the complication caused by finance. If it is your passion to make the human race bound for the stars and reside on other planets, then you will always have a place with us. There are others who are passionate about this too, and we will work to give you whatever you need to make this happen because personally, I want it to happen too and I believe I would be willing to work for such a cause, especially if it meant I could get more public trading system hours to ask for things I want in return. I would do a good job because I believe in it, just as I have written this book to express my idea because I believe in it. There are so many people who believe that a space program is a noble endeavor, that you would likely just get anything you need to build your space vehicles. You won't have a

Karactus Blome

budget, you will only be limited by what your volunteer suppliers can take from the Earth. Since all of us volunteer, our employment rate will always be 100%. Participating in the system is what makes you a citizen. If you don't work, you won't be a citizen. Citizenship in our country is as easy as to obtain as creating an entry for yourself in our database. Put your name and what you want your profession to be, and you're in. That's it! Then you just start working and racking up public trading system time to make requests on it. Even before we acquire the assets we need to be our own country, if you have ideas please put them forward as tasks on the public trading system. You can make free requests on the public trading system in the time before we become a real country. If others think your requests are good ideas, they will likely happen because there is a consensus among people in the professions your request concerns who agree with it, or there are people who can join the involved professions to work on it if they want, after learning how to do so of course.

The whole time we are gathering the momentum

The Proletarianist Manifesto, 3rd Edition

we need to break away, we should be running a fundraiser. Anyone who wants to see proletarianism happen will of course be free to contribute to it.

Once we have enough people on board with us and achieve our goal with the fundraiser, the next phase of our plan begins. We could likely do it when we have support from a quarter of a given country's population, provided that we have people from all sorts of professions. At this point, we will take the money we obtained through the fundraiser to buy some land from capitalists or perhaps the country's government. This is the point at which we break off from the society that already exists in the country, and actually construct our own on the land we buy. We will relocate the computers for the public trading system on this land, and zone it for maximum economic efficiency, as described in Section II. We will need many professions in on this, so I will make this my next public trading system request: allocate and zone our land for the production of whatever resources we find on it. This will call for a huge survey of our land and what resources are on it. Any flat plains with fertile soil should clearly be

Karactus Blome

allocated for farming. Wherever there is metal, there will be mines. Wherever there is forest is where we will build our logging communities. Where there is water is where we shall obtain it. Wherever there are any resources, there will be a community with workers trained to obtain them and use them to produce other things.

Note that at this point in the process, we will not yet have officially seceded from our parent country in which the land resides.

You will all know the principles by which our new country will operate; all of those free tasks you asked for in the time before the we broke away are now the first jobs in our economy. You have expressed passion for these things by requesting them, now take whatever resources you need from the land and go do these jobs. Accept a task on the public trading system and start working; our first generation of people living under proletarianism will have been educated by whatever school system the old society had in place before we broke away; this is okay. This is the knowledge we will have to work with at first, so you will likely sign on for a similar profession that the

The Proletarianist Manifesto, 3rd Edition

capitalists paid you for (unless you don't like it, in which case by all means try changing it up).

I am now placing another request: build the education system according to Section II. This request concerns any professions we think will be involved in this. By placing this request, I am also creating our first teaching jobs. Teachers shall be given the same treatment as any other profession on the system. They work for public trading system time too, and are simply passionate about rearing the young to be successful. This request is called for out of necessity if nothing else. We need to prepare future generations to work in our new society, period. I'm sure this request will be carried out because I am rather certain most people are in agreement that we need to educate our people. If you get any requests from schools on the public trading system that concern your profession, it will likely just be in your best interest to accept them, but I probably didn't even have to tell you that because you already know.

At this point, we will need to build our army. Any soldiers who signed on with us shall be welcomed with

Karactus Blome

open arms. To those in the military who side with us, thank you for actually siding with the people for once and not our corrupt government. Unfortunately, we might require your services pretty soon. Make use of the public trading system to tell us whatever you need to defend our country, and we will do our best to provide what you need. If you need fortifications built, no problem. Personally, I would volunteer to help build them if I was of any professions such a task involves, and I am sure others would too because I have reason to believe we will need to defend ourselves against retaliation from the old system very soon. Arm yourselves, everyone. We must prepare to make a stand if war comes our way.

By now, proletarianism is officially established. At this point, we declare independence and secede. If the old system's power hasn't already diminished beyond the ability take action against us, it will likely try to stop us. We can hope that the old system will go peacefully, but it would seem unlikely. Once in power, people tend to want to stay in power, so do not expect this to go unopposed by the old system. I hope we can work this out peacefully

The Proletarianist Manifesto, 3rd Edition

with the old government but they might not want to let go, in which case they will come for us. If they do, we must all stand together to fight our oppressors. The future of the nation shall depend on the outcome of this sacred war if it comes to it. We must defend our new homeland at all costs. Do not try to invade any territory still controlled by the government, for we will lose any support we have from the international community. I cannot stress this enough! Stay in our territory and only defend what we already have. Here comes the government, trying to force its corruption on us; we cannot tolerate it, so send those pigs straight to hell! Open fire! Don't stop firing until all of the goons the enemy sends surrender or lie dead in a pool of their own blood; those are your orders, soldiers.

    If the war happens, we defend ourselves. I hope the officials under the old system will listen to voices of reason and simply let us go (we really aren't worth it), but this is unlikely because many humans just don't care and want to hold onto their power over as many people as they can.

    All we are trying to do is live our own lives the

Karactus Blome

way we want to, with the help of everyone else who joins with us. We won't deliberately start any trouble with other nations, but we will defend ourselves if we really need to.

The Proletarianist Manifesto, 3rd Edition

Conclusions

For those of you who are still reading, thank you very much for your patience. I'm sure you might still have questions. I have already laid out how we will address people's concerns.

I admit that I am not able to solve every problem with this system that others bring up, but I imagine that someone will probably come along and request a solution to your problem on the public trading system (if you don't take it upon yourself to do so). Another one of us with the necessary knowledge or insight will likely be able to address your problem to the satisfaction of everyone it concerns even if I can't.

My goal here was not to create a perfect country. I admit that, like any other system, proletarianism will not be without its own set of problems. I am only one person, and try as I might, I will not be able to solve everyone's problems in one sweeping resolution. However I have provided the framework for a system that will make every attempt to find and experiment with solutions to most problems we encounter, and that's good enough for me.

Karactus Blome

Whatever our problems are, I am certain we can work together to figure something out that works.

You might have noticed that I have not discussed religion at all. This is because I think that with all of the problems the human race is having at the time of this writing, we have better things to do with our time than to be thinking about things we will never prove. Is there a higher power? Should we believe there is? I can't answer that question for you. I can tell you what I personally believe and you can tell me what you personally believe, but in the end such things are for the individual to decide. If you really feel the need convince others that your beliefs are right and that everyone else is wrong, then it can wait until we are dead as I am sure we will know the truth then, and you can brag about it all you want if you turn out to be right. At this point though, I fail to understand how people know, or why they even care whether or not there is a higher power.

We are not a leftist or a rightist movement. We are not socialists. We are not communists. We are not capitalists, nor are we syndicalists or anarchists. We are

The Proletarianist Manifesto, 3rd Edition

not looking at the bank account statements or the symbolic dollar amounts that our capitalist friends are obsessed with. We are proletarianists. We are looking directly at what physically exists and deciding what we want to do with it, which is what really matters. Telling us to leave your country if we don't like how it runs is pointless. You should already know what we want to do and if you don't want to join us, then our plan will not affect you. If you want to stay here with the rest of these fools, arguing about how much we're spending or cutting or how high you think taxes should be, then fine. That is your decision. We will already be living on other planets by the time those idiots are finished punching numbers on their calculators to find out how much money it would cost to get out there. Just remember that.

We are not forcing you to join us. We are not going to force our system on you or anyone else. We are going to do what we want, and we are leaving the rest of you behind. Plain and simple.

You can sit there while you're reading this and bitch about how you think a lack of government would result in barbarism or how you think we can't get rid of the money system and how you think we would be bartering even if we did (because God forbid we can't be creative and try anything new, right?), but such things are only what you believe you know. No one knows for sure if proletarianism will work until someone tries it. You can believe you know anything, but it doesn't mean you really know it.

All of this being said, those of you who want to take this evolutionary step to become better than what we've ever been are free to join us. You know exactly what needs to happen. Let us commence with all due haste, and prove the others wrong. Humanity is better than what we were taught to believe it is and we can prove it together. A shout-out to everyone else who agrees:

FORWARD! LET'S GO!

The Proletarianist Manifesto, 3rd Edition

www.ingramcontent.com/pod-product-compliance
Lightning Source LLC
Chambersburg PA
CBHW071806170526
45167CB00003B/1191